LIVING IN... MEXICO

by Chloe Perkins
illustrated by Tom Woolley

READY-TO-READ

SIMON SPOTLIGHT

An imprint of Simon & Schuster Children's Publishing Division • New York   London   Toronto   Sydney   New Delhi • 1230 Avenue of the Americas, New York, New York 10020 • This Simon Spotlight edition September 2017 • Text copyright © 2016 by Simon & Schuster, Inc. Illustrations copyright © 2016 by Tom Woolley • All rights reserved, including the right of reproduction in whole or in part in any form. SIMON SPOTLIGHT, READY-TO-READ, and colophon are registered trademarks of Simon & Schuster, Inc. For information about special discounts for bulk purchases, please contact Simon & Schuster Special Sales at 1-866-506-1949 or business@simonandschuster.com. Manufactured in China 0118 SDI

GLOSSARY

Aztecs: the Native Mexican people who lived in and ruled much of central and southern Mexico from the 1400s to 1519 CE

BCE/CE: how years are measured by the Western calendar; BCE stands for "Before the Common Era" and the year increases as it is further back in time; CE stands for "Common Era" and the year increases as it is further forward in time

Colony: a place that is taken over and controlled by a faraway country

Conquer: to take control of a place or a group of people by force

Folk art: art, such as carving, basketry, or painting, that is created by common people to reflect their culture

Mayans: the Native Mexican people who lived in Mexico and other parts of North and Central America from 1500 BCE to 900 CE

Olmecs: the Native Mexican people who lived in southern Mexico from 1200 BCE to 400 BCE

Peninsula: a piece of land that is surrounded by water on three sides

Plateau: a flat area of land that is raised higher than the land around it

Pyramid: a large structure built with a square base and four sides that come together to form a point at the top

Temple: a building used to practice one's religion

NOTE TO READERS: Some of these words may have more than one definition. The definitions above are how these words are used in this book.

¡Hola! (say: OH-la)
That means "hi" in Spanish.
My name is Rosa,
and I live in Mexico.
Mexico is a country in
North America where more
than one hundred and twenty
million people live . . .
including me!

Mexico is a beautiful country. Many people come here to visit the pretty beaches and deserts, or to hike in the rain forests and mountains.

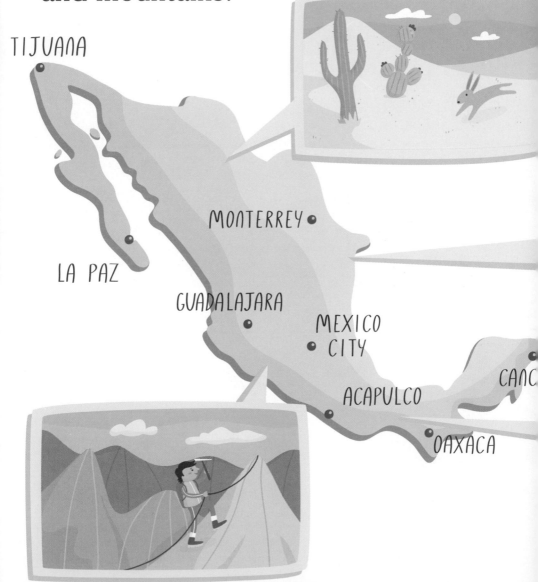

TIJUANA

LA PAZ

MONTERREY

GUADALAJARA

MEXICO CITY

ACAPULCO

CANC

OAXACA

The weather in Mexico
is very different from place
to place. Near the ocean
and rain forest, the weather
is hot and humid.
In the mountains and
on the plateau, the weather is
dry and mild.

Mexico has two big deserts in the north. The deserts are home to many plants and animals, such as roadrunners, mountain lions, and cactuses that can grow up to sixty feet tall!

Two mountain ranges
run down Mexico's east
and west sides.
Between the mountains
is the Mexican Plateau.
Many people live
on the plateau.

Mexico's capital city, Mexico City,
is on the plateau. It was built
on top of an ancient city.
Guadalajara (say: gwah-dah-lah-HAH-rah)
holds a yearly festival for a
special kind of Mexican music,
called mariachi (say: mah-ree-AH-chee).

GUADALAJARA

Cancún (say: kahn-KOON) has some
of the best beaches in the world.
Oaxaca (say: wah-HAH-kah)
is home to colorful
festivals and folk art.

I live in La Paz, a city on the Baja (say: bah-ha) California Peninsula of Mexico. I live with my mom, dad, brother, and sister.

LA PAZ

My parents work for a sailing
company. They take people
on sailboats to see the
gray whales.
I love watching the whales.
I want to study whales
when I grow up.

Every morning I get ready
for school.
I brush my teeth and
put on my school uniform.

Then I comb my hair neatly.
In Mexico it's important to look
neat and clean for school.

For breakfast we
eat fried eggs,
beans, and sauce on
a tortilla (say: tor-TEE-yah).
A tortilla is a round,
flat piece of bread.

After breakfast
my mom and dad drive
me to school.
My brother and sister
go to a school for
younger kids.

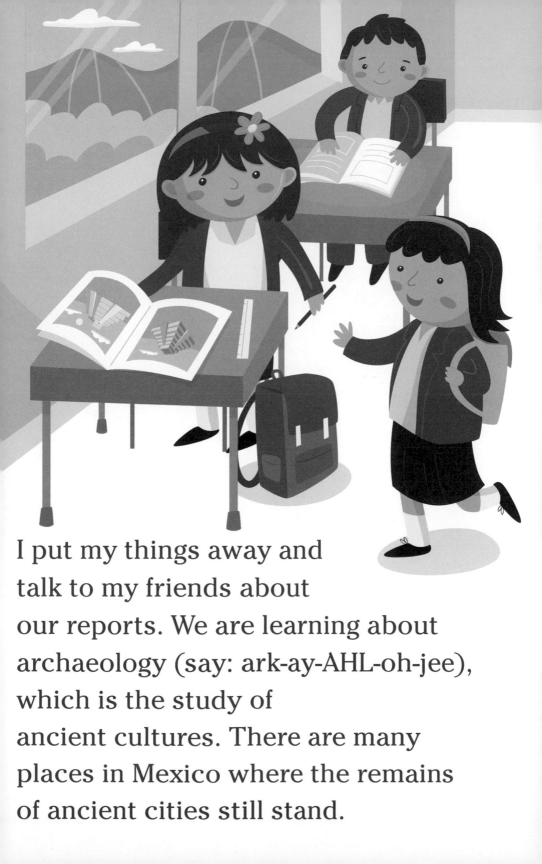

I put my things away and
talk to my friends about
our reports. We are learning about
archaeology (say: ark-ay-AHL-oh-jee),
which is the study of
ancient cultures. There are many
places in Mexico where the remains
of ancient cities still stand.

School starts at
eight o'clock each
morning. The first half
of the day is taught
in Spanish. After snack time
we are taught in English.
I speak both languages!

Our first lesson in Spanish is about Mexico's history. Ten thousand years ago, people in the region started coming together to farm the land.

In 1500 BCE the Olmec (say: OL-mek)
people began growing
many things we have today,
such as corn, beans, and cotton.
Around 600 BCE, the Olmecs split
into different groups, one of
which was the Mayans (say: MY-ans).

Between 1325 CE and 1519 CE
the Aztec people conquered
many groups and
brought them together.
The Aztecs built
pyramids and temples,
created jewelry and art,
and lived in huge cities.

In 1519 CE, Hernán Cortés,
a European explorer, was sent
to claim the Aztecs' land for Spain.
In 1521 he succeeded.
The Spanish conquered more
and more people and took
their land. They called the
colony "New Spain."

Spain ruled for almost three hundred years. But the people of New Spain wanted their own country.
They wanted to be free.
They fought many battles with Spain.
The people won their freedom in 1821, and "New Spain" became Mexico!

After our history lesson
we have a snack.
Today's snack is juicy
pineapple sprinkled with
chili powder and lime juice.
After we clean up,
we start our math lesson
in English.

I really like math. Look!
I got a ten on my math test!
In Mexico we are graded
with numbers instead of letters.
A ten is the best score
you can get.

We have geography and science lessons, and then school is over at two o'clock! My family picks me up for lunch. In Mexico lunch is the most important meal of the day. My parents have a break from work to eat.

For lunch we are eating
quesadillas (say: kay-sah-DEE-yahs).
Quesadillas are like a sandwich.
Cheese, beans, and chicken
go on top of a tortilla.
Then you put another tortilla
on top and cook it.
As we eat, we talk about our day.

After lunch my brother, sister, and I go to our after-school programs. In Mexico many kids attend after-school programs while their parents work. My little brother and sister play soccer.

I take a special art class for
older kids. We're learning about
Diego Rivera and Frida Kahlo,
two famous Mexican artists
from the 1900s.
Our parents pick us up when their
work is over, and we go home.

In Mexico we have a
holiday in November
called the Day of the Dead.
We celebrate the lives
of family and friends
who have died.
There are big parades
and celebrations!

I help my mom make a special bread. We will eat it at the parade tomorrow. My brother and sister put up pretty paper banners to decorate the house for the holiday.

Dinnertime! In Mexico
dinner is usually
a light meal.
Tonight we're having
chilled avocado soup.

Before bed I read my book about whales, fish, and dolphins around the world. Someday I'm going to sail to different countries and see them. Would you like to visit Mexico someday?

ALL ABOUT
MEXICO!

NAME: United Mexican States (Or Mexico for short!)

POPULATION: 122 million

CAPITAL: Mexico City

LANGUAGE: primarily Spanish, though the government recognizes sixty eight indigenous languages, including Nahuatl, Yucatec Mayan, and Mixtec

TOTAL AREA: 758,449 square miles

GOVERNMENT: federal republic

CURRENCY: peso

FUN FACT: Chocolate originated in Mexico roughly four thousand years ago! Starting around 1900 BCE ancient people living in Mexico ground cacao beans down and added them to a mix of vanilla, honey, chili peppers, and water. The result was the first hot chocolate, a special drink reserved for rulers, wealthy nobles, and warriors!

FLAG: three equal-size vertical stripes of green, white, and red–Mexico's coat of arms, an eagle with a snake in its mouth standing on a cactus, appears in the center